# John Thompson's Easiest Piano Course

## PART FOUR

Exclusive distributors:
Music Sales Limited, 8-9 Frith Street, London W1V 5TZ.
Music Sales Pty Limited, 120 Rothschild Avenue, Rosebery, NSW 2018, Australia.

Order No. WMR000320

Unauthorised reproduction of any part of this publication by any
means including photocopying is an infringement of copyright.

Printed and bound in the United Kingdom by Printwise (Haverhill) Limited, Haverhill, Suffolk.

This publication is not for sale in the
United States of America and/or Canada

The Willis Music Co.

© Copyright 1956 & 1996 The Willis Music Company, Florence, Kentucky, USA.
All Rights Reserved.

# Foreword

The primary purpose of PART FOUR is to allow the pupil opportunity to develop efficiency and fluency in the application of knowledge gained in the earlier books. For that reason, there are not many new demands made in a technical way. Several new Keys are introduced, namely, E Major, B Major, A Flat Major, D Flat Major and G Flat Major. The examples in the new Keys are purposely kept simple. Leger Lines between the staves are also presented with charts showing an easy way to recognize notes written on the added lines. The dotted crotchet is explained and examples given in Three-Four and Four-Four. There are also examples in which a change of fingers is required when playing repeated notes. This, of course, results in an extension of hand position and prepares the way for passing the Thumb under and the Hand over—a phase of technique taken up in Part Five. Simple, most elementary use of the Pedal is allowed in some of the later pieces and prepares the pupil for detailed study of the art of pedalling which is also taken up in Part Five.

In general, PART FOUR, except for the points outlined above, is mostly a book of review work. It should afford the pupil a chance to enjoy the fruits of his labour to date, and at the same time develop better pianism, musicianship and general musical understanding.

When this book is finished, the student will be ready for another advance in technique and the following book will contain material with more extended passage playing. Meantime, every effort should be made to play the examples in this book with the best possible artistry.

*John Thompson*

# Contents

| | Page |
|---|---|
| **FOREWORD** | 3 |
| **WRIST STACCATO**—"Dancing Raindrops" | 5 |
| **MELODY IN THE LEFT HAND** "At the Ball" | 6 |
| **LEGER LINES ABOVE BASS STAFF** | 8 |
| **ETUDE ON LEGER LINES** | 9 |
| **DOTTED CROTCHETS in THREE-FOUR** "Song of the Brook" | 10 |
| **DOTTED CROTCHETS in FOUR-FOUR** "Puck" | 11 |
| **LEGER LINES BELOW TREBLE STAFF** | 12 |
| **ETUDE ON LEGER LINES** | 13 |
| **FINGER CHANGE ON THE SAME KEY** "From a Story Book" | 14 |
| "Comin' 'Round the Mountain" | 15 |
| **WORK SHEET**—New Key—E MAJOR | 16 |
| **FIVE-FINGER DRILL IN E MAJOR** "Cotton-pickin' Fingers" | 17 |
| **TWO AND THREE-NOTE SLURS** "Barcarolle" from "The Tales of Hoffmann" . . . . Offenbach | 18 |
| **SHORT AND LONG SLURS** "The Cuckoo Clock" | 19 |
| **STACCATO THIRDS** "The Overland Stage" | 20 |
| **WORK SHEET**—New Key—A FLAT MAJOR | 21 |
| **BROKEN CHORD STUDY IN A FLAT MAJOR** "Giant Redwood Trees" | 22 |

| | Page |
|---|---|
| **STACCATO STUDY**—from the Opera "William Tell" . . . G. Rossini | 24 |
| **RECITAL PIECE**—from "The Beautiful Blue Danube" . . . Johann Strauss | 26 |
| **CROSS-HAND PIECE** "Scampering Squirrels" | 28 |
| **SYNCOPATION**—"College Capers" | 29 |
| **WORK SHEET**—New Key—B MAJOR | 30 |
| **STUDY IN B MAJOR**—"Bohemian Dance" | 31 |
| **NOCTURNE**—"Song of Twilight" | 32 |
| **STACCATO AND SOSTENUTO** from "Hopak" Modest P. Moussorgsky | 33 |
| **WORK SHEET**—New Key—D FLAT MAJOR | 34 |
| **ETUDE IN D FLAT MAJOR** | 35 |
| **RECITAL PIECE**—"At the Skating Rink" | 36 |
| **WORK SHEET**—New Key—G FLAT MAJOR | 38 |
| **STUDY IN G FLAT MAJOR** "Korean Serenade" | 39 |
| **NOVELTY**—"The Man on the Flying Trapeze" Anon. 1868 | 40 |
| **RECITAL PIECE** from "Narcissus" Ethelbert Nevin | 42 |
| **GLOSSARY OF MUSICAL TERMS** | 45 |
| **NEW SCALES AND CHORDS** | 46 |
| **CERTIFICATE** | 47 |

# Wrist Staccato

TEACHER'S NOTE: This number should be played with a bouncing wrist staccato. For development of the various Touches, assign John Thompson's HANON STUDIES, specially designed for use in this grade.

## Dancing Raindrops

# Melody in the Left Hand

In this piece, the melody lies in the left hand.

Try to play it with your best singing tone while the right hand supplies a light, staccato accompaniment of familiar chord patterns, learned earlier in the Course.

## At the Ball

# Leger Lines
## (Above the Bass Staff)

Leger Lines are little lines added above or below the staff upon which to write additional notes.

The Leger Lines <u>above</u> the Bass Staff are easy to read if it is remembered that all lines <u>above</u> **Middle C** are really Treble Lines, <u>borrowed</u> <u>and</u> <u>brought</u> <u>down</u> for use as Leger Lines.

Example:

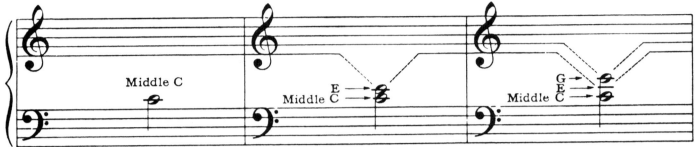

These notes in Treble Clef ——— when transposed to Bass Clef ——— look like this on the music.

# Writing Exercises

Write the letter-names under these notes, then transpose them to Treble Clef.

Transpose these notes to the Bass Clef, using Leger Lines.

Remember that all added lines <u>above</u> Middle C are <u>borrowed</u> from the Treble and brought down as Leger Lines.

## Etude on Leger Lines

# Dotted Crotchets
## (In Three-Four)

You have already played dotted minims and learned how the dot adds an extra <u>half</u> <u>value</u> to each note so marked.

A dotted crotchet will be equal to one full count <u>plus</u> <u>one</u> <u>half</u> <u>of</u> <u>the</u> <u>next</u> <u>count</u>.

If you imagine a Tie connecting the full count to the next half count, it will be easy to play.

Example:

# Leger Lines
## (Below the Treble Staff)

The Leger Lines below the Treble Staff are easy to read if it is remembered that all lines <u>below</u> <u>Middle C</u> are really Bass Lines, <u>borrowed</u> and <u>brought</u> <u>up</u> for use as Leger Lines.

Example:

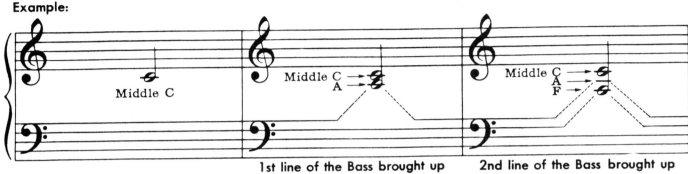

# Writing Exercises

Write the letter-names over these notes, then transpose them to Bass Clef.

Transpose these notes to the Treble Clef, using Leger Lines.

Remember that all added lines <u>below</u> Middle C are Bass Lines, <u>borrowed</u> and used as Leger Lines in the Treble.

# Etude on Leger Lines

# Finger Change on the Same Key

A change of fingers when a key is repeated, results automatically in a new Hand Position, thus increasing the number of keys lying within reach of the fingers.

Watch the fingering carefully in the following example.

## From a Story Book

# Work Sheet
## New Key — E Major

E MAJOR has four sharps — F# C# G# D#.

Write the E Major Scale, using accidentals as necessary to preserve the scale pattern.

Remember that semitones occur only between the 3rd and 4th and 7th and 8th degrees of the scale. All others are whole tones.

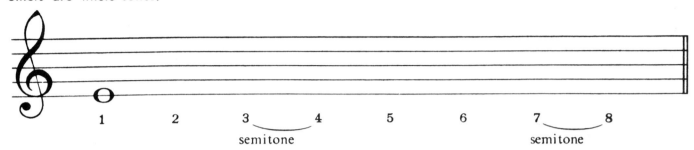

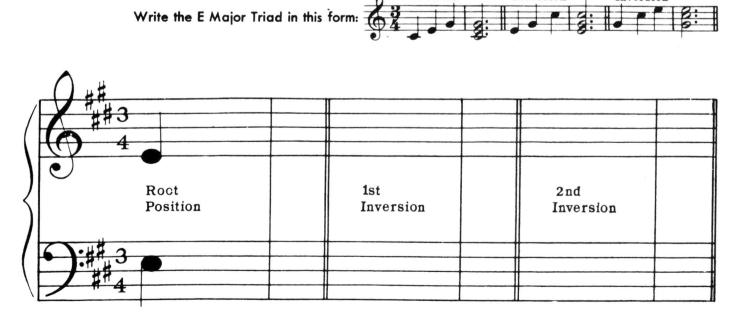

# Five-Finger Drill in E Major
## Cotton-pickin' Fingers

Be sure to make a distinction between the slurred groups and staccato notes in this piece.

# Two and Three-note Slurs

Be sure to observe the Two and Three-note slurs. When they are played correctly, they will imitate the rocking motion of a Gondola as it glides over the waters of a Venetian canal.

## Barcarolle

from "The Tales of Hoffmann"

J. Offenbach

# Short and Long Slurs

## The Cuckoo Clock

# Staccato Thirds

Sostenuto is a musical term meaning "in a sustained manner." A note or chord to be played thus is often indicated by a little line placed above or below it like this, 𝅘𝅥 or 𝄖.

In the following piece, see how much contrast you can make between the chords marked staccato and those having the sostenuto sign.

## The Overland Stage

# Work Sheet
## New Key — A♭ Major

A FLAT MAJOR has four flats — B♭ E♭ A♭ D♭.

Write the A flat Major Scale using accidentals as necessary to preserve the scale pattern.

Remember that semitones occur only between the 3rd and 4th and 7th and 8th degrees of the scale. All others are whole tones.

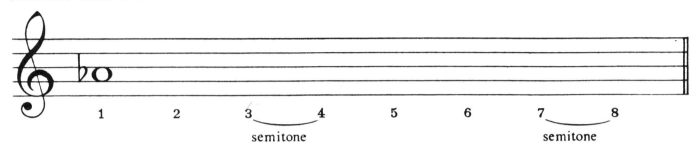

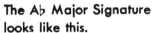

The A♭ Major Signature looks like this.

Copy it here.

Write the A♭ Major Triad in this form:

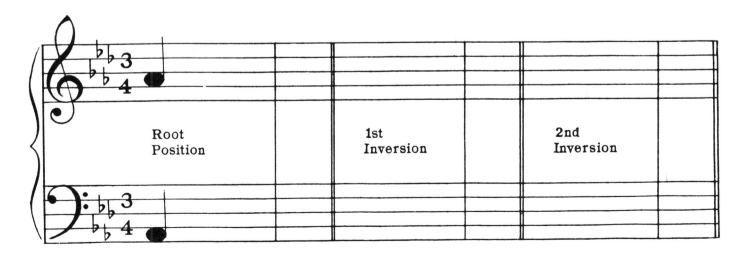

Root Position     1st Inversion     2nd Inversion

W.M.Co. 7339

# Broken Chord Study in A Flat Major

**TEACHER'S NOTE:** While the art of Pedalling has not yet been presented (it will be given in detail later in the Course) it seems advisable to allow its use in simple, elementary form in this piece as well as in some others which follow, especially as extended arpeggio passages are rather lifeless without it.

It will suffice at this point to explain to the pupil that the damper (right) pedal is pressed down at the word, "Ped." and is held until the star (✻) appears, when it is immediately released.

## Giant Redwood Trees

# Staccato Study

**TEACHER'S NOTE:** The following piece may be played with either wrist or finger staccato. If wrist staccato is used, the repeated notes are played with the same finger. Whereas if finger staccato is employed, it calls for a change of finger on each note. For this reason, two sets of fingering are given.

For full description of the various staccato Touches (finger, wrist, forearm) see John Thompson's HANON STUDIES.

## from the Opera "William Tell"

G. Rossini

# Syncopation

> To produce a syncopated effect, be sure to apply heavy accents as marked.

## College Capers

Allegro moderato

# Work Sheet
## New Key — B Major

B MAJOR has five sharps — F# C# G# D# A#.

Write the B Major Scale, using accidentals as necessary to preserve the scale pattern.

Remember that semitones occur only between the 3rd and 4th and 7th and 8th degrees of the scale. All others are whole tones.

# Study in B Major

## Bohemian Dance

NOCTURNE means Night Song. It is a form of composition often used and always consists of a lyric piece with a mood suggesting the quiet of evening.

# Song of Twilight

**Nocturne**

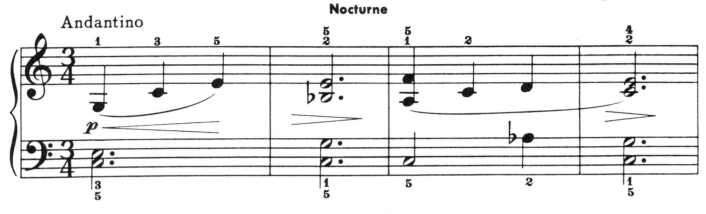
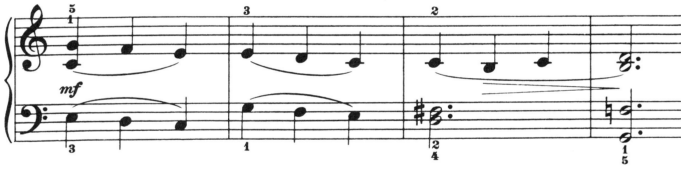

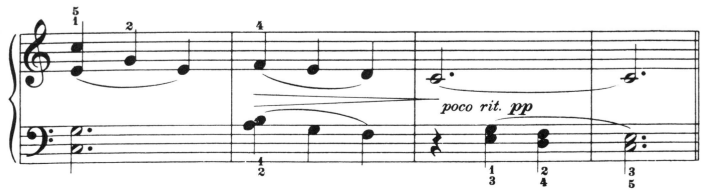

# Staccato and Sostenuto

Play this dance with plenty of fire and dash.

Apply sharp staccatos, heavy accents and watch for the occasional <u>sostenuto</u> marks.

from
## Hopak
Modest P. Moussorgsky

# Work Sheet
## New Key—D♭ Major

D FLAT MAJOR has five flats — B♭ E♭ A♭ D♭ G♭.

Write the D flat Major Scale, using accidentals as necessary to preserve the scale pattern.

Remember that semitones occur only between the 3rd and 4th and 7th and 8th degrees of the scale. All others are whole tones.

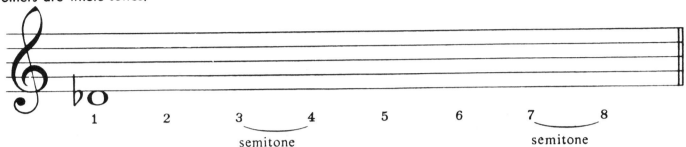

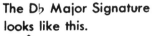

Write the D♭ Major Triad in this form:

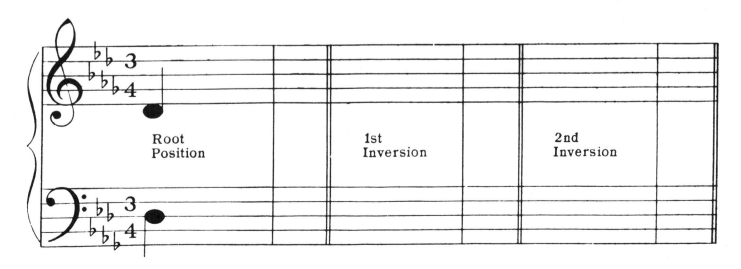

W.M.Co. 7339

# Etude in D Flat Major

# At the Skating Rink

# Work Sheet
## New Key—G♭ Major

G FLAT MAJOR has six flats — B♭ E♭ A♭ D♭ G♭ C♭.

Write the G flat Major Scale, using accidentals as necessary to preserve the scale pattern.

Remember that semitones occur only between the 3rd and 4th and 7th and 8th degrees of the scale. All others are whole tones.

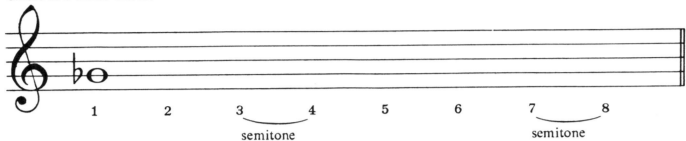

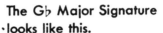

**The G♭ Major Signature looks like this.**

**Copy it here.**

Write the G♭ Major Triad in this form:

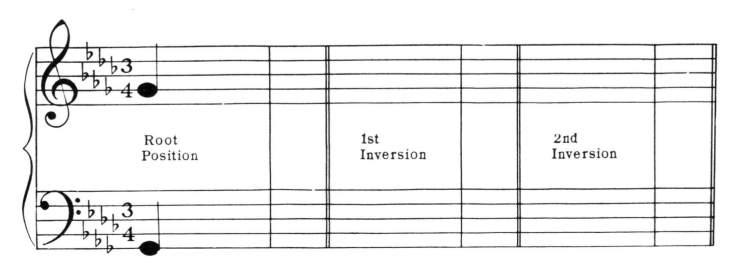

# Study in G Flat Major

## Korean Serenade

Watch for the new flat (C♭). It occurs only once. Be sure to find it!

# The Man on the Flying Trapeze

Anon. 1868

# Narcissus

from

Ethelbert Nevin

# GLOSSARY

## of

### Musical Terms and Expression Marks
### Used in this book.

> — Accent ... Special emphasis on a note or chord

**Allegretto** ... Light and Lively

**Allegro** ... Fast

**Andante** ... Slow

**Andantino** ... Slow, but not as slow as Andante

**Animato** ... Animated

**a tempo** ... Return to original speed

⊂ — Crescendo ... Gradually louder

⊃ — Decrescendo ... Gradually softer

**Diminuendo** ... Softer by degrees

*f* — Forte ... Loud

*ff* — Fortissimo ... Very loud

**Legato** ... Smooth and connected

**L.H.** ... Left Hand

*8-------* Play one octave higher

*mf* — Mezzo Forte ... Moderately loud

*mp* — Mezzo Piano ... Moderately soft

**Moderato** ... Moderately fast

⌒ — Pause ... Hold the note or chord longer according to taste

*pp* — Pianissimo ... Very soft

*p* — Piano ... Soft

**Poco** ... Little

Repeat Sign

**R.H.** ... Right Hand

**Rit** ... **Ritard** ... Slower by degrees

⌒ — Slur ... Connected

**Staccato** ... Detached, short

**Tempo** ... Rate of speed

**Vivace** ... Fast and vivacious

# New Scales and Chords

# Certificate of Merit

This certifies that

..................................................................................

has successfully completed

**PART FOUR**

OF

**John Thompson's**

**EASIEST PIANO COURSE**

and is eligible for promotion to

**PART FIVE**

..................................................................................
*Teacher*

Date ..................................................................